Amazing Engineers

VISTA®
HIGHER LEARNING

Boston, Massachusetts

SCIENCE

They save us hours of time. They make our homes and buildings safer. Their work makes our daily lives easier and more convenient. They help entertain us, and they keep us in touch with our friends and families who live far away. Our lives are better and more interesting in thousands of ways because of them. In fact, they may even save the world someday. Who are these superheroes? Engineers, of course!

UNBALANCED
BALANCED
results
DIRECTION
MOTION
MASS
force PUSH
STRENGTH
PULL

Engineers can do incredible things, but their jobs aren't easy. They need to study advanced math and sciences, such as calculus and physics. They must understand how **forces**, **mass**, and **motion** work together. They perform **investigations** to find answers and test ideas.

Then, engineers use what they've learned to design things, build things, and make things better. They develop and fix computers, machines, buildings, bridges, and a whole lot more. Let's take a look at some of the work of amazing engineers!

1 mile = 1.6 km; 1 ton = 907 kg

Marin County

San Francisco

This famous bridge saves people hours of travel time every day. It allows them to drive safely over San Francisco Bay and the Pacific Ocean. It's the Golden Gate Bridge in California, and it connects the city of San Francisco to Marin County.

This type of bridge is called a suspension bridge. It's 1.7 miles long and weighs 887,000 tons. It was built between 1933 and 1937. At the time it was completed, it was the longest and tallest bridge of its kind in the world!

side to side

collapse

Obviously, all bridges need to be strong and safe. But a long, tall bridge like the Golden Gate is especially difficult to build and **maintain**. It must be able to support its own weight. It must also support the weight of the vehicles that cross it. Over 100,000 cars, buses, and trucks drive over the Golden Gate Bridge every day!

In the case of the Golden Gate Bridge, there are also strong winds that push the bridge from side to side. The engineers who designed it had to think about all of these forces that would act upon the bridge. They had to make sure that the forces wouldn't become **unbalanced**. If they did, the bridge would **collapse**!

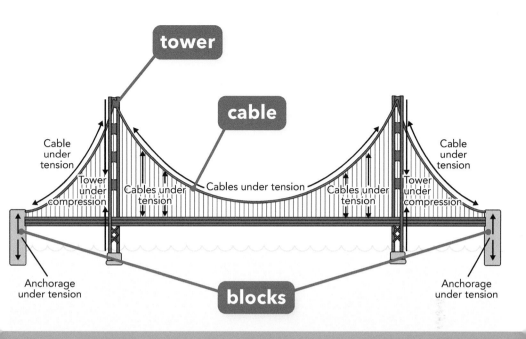

tower

cable

Cable under tension

Tower under compression

Cables under tension

Cables under tension

Cables under tension

Tower under compression

Cable under tension

Anchorage under tension

blocks

Anchorage under tension

The Golden Gate Bridge is held up by strong cables. The cables are held in place by tall towers and heavy blocks called "anchorages." The anchorages for the cables are located at each end of the bridge.

The weight of the bridge with the cars and the wind moving it side to side create forces on the bridge. This results in a force in the cables called **tension**. This tension is transferred through the cables into the towers and anchorages. It then goes into the ground. All the forces in the structure are balanced.

If the towers and anchorages weren't strong enough, the bridge would simply collapse. This is why engineers are so important. They do the calculations needed to keep these forces balanced. Engineers make sure that the bridge is safe!

Bridges are important for traveling over water. However, to travel under the ground, we need tunnels. This is the Gotthard Base Tunnel in Switzerland. It's one of the longest and deepest train tunnels in the world, and it was extremely difficult to build.

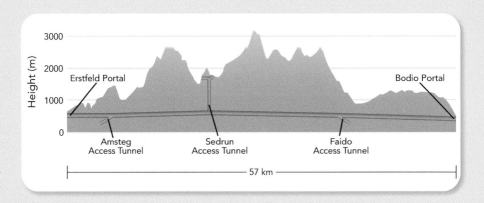

Workers had to cut through 35 miles (57 km) of rock under huge mountains. They used large tunneling machines to do this. To save time, they cut from both ends of the tunnel at the same time. They also cut access tunnels in the middle that went through the mountains. This way, more tunneling machines could dig in different places at the same time.

The Gotthard Base Tunnel was a very dangerous project as well. There were huge masses of rock above the tunnel. The force of **gravity** was always at work. This meant that there was always the danger of a tunnel collapse.

To keep the rock from falling, engineers put strong metal rings in the tunnel. They used complicated math **calculations** to figure out how much strength the rings needed. They had to be sure the rings could balance the forces of the heavy rock.

Another problem engineers faced was the high temperatures deep in the tunnel. At times, temperatures could reach up to 111°F (44°C). Engineers needed to build special machines to cool work areas down.

The finished tunnel opened in 2016. It has proved to be well worth the effort. People can now travel quickly and easily by train through the mountains. They no longer have to drive around or over them. Trains also carry products, so fewer trucks are needed on the roads. Using the tunnel has proven to be both faster and better for the environment.

KNOW IT ALL

Engineers on the Gotthard Base Tunnel worked hard to make conditions safe. However some accidents did happen. During the 17 years it took to complete it, nine workers lost their lives.

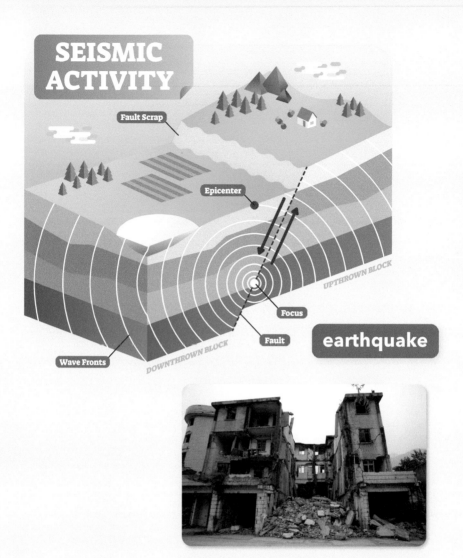

So, we now know that engineers help us travel more safely and quickly from place to place. Now let's look at how engineers make our homes and workplaces better and safer.

Many areas of the world experience earthquakes. They're usually small, but when they're powerful, earthquakes can be very dangerous. The motion of the earth can damage buildings. It can even cause them to collapse. People can be badly hurt or lose their homes as a result.

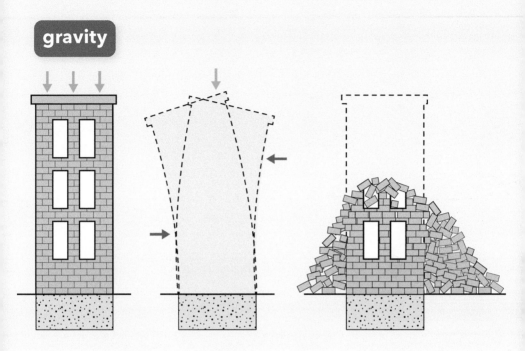

gravity

Most buildings are built to **resist** the normal downward pull of gravity. Their walls and floors have the strength to balance the forces of gravity. As a result, buildings don't collapse because of their own weight.

Earthquakes, however, create a different kind of force. While gravity pulls down, earthquakes move the ground from side to side. The walls of buildings usually can't move this way. They can't balance the forces of the earthquake. This motion can cause walls to break and buildings to collapse.

11

This building, however, is different. It's called the Torre Reforma, and it's one of the tallest buildings in Mexico City. Torre Reforma was built between 2008 and 2016. Mexico can have powerful earthquakes. Because of this, engineers designed the building with walls that can move and bend without breaking. The walls and floors are able to take in and balance the forces of an earthquake. The building is much less likely to suffer major damage because of this. In fact, a huge earthquake hit Mexico City in 2017. The Torre Reforma stood tall while some smaller, older buildings collapsed.

EXTRA!

It's eco-friendly. It's safe and helpful for the environment and the people in it.

TORRE REFORMA FACTS

- Engineers tested the design of Torre Reforma on computers before building the tower. They created computer models of earthquake events. This showed them what would happen to the building in an earthquake.

- The walls of the building reach 197 feet (60 meters) under the ground. This helps support the weight of the building and keep it standing during an earthquake.

- In addition to being safe, the Torre Reforma is also eco-friendly. Engineers designed it to save energy and recycle water. It even has gardens inside!

So, You Want to Be an Engineer?

Good for you! There isn't just one type of engineer, though. In fact, there are many different areas of engineering you can choose from. Here is information about four general areas of engineering and some of the work engineers in those fields do.

Civil engineering: deal with buildings, public works, and systems such as water systems, tunnels, bridges, roads, and so on

Chemical engineering: use chemistry and biology for research and making products

Electrical engineering: deal with electrical systems, electronics, computer systems, and networks

Mechanical engineering: handle the design, building, and testing of machines and systems that use or produce machines

Many types of engineers fall under each general area. Some engineering jobs combine elements from more than one area. What kind of engineer would you like to be?

- Do you want to help save Earth? Would you like to develop systems that protect living things? Why not become an environmental engineer?

- How about designing new and better cars? You could be an automotive engineer.

- Do airplanes and spaceships sound more exciting? Maybe you should be an aerospace engineer!

- Would you like to help people with difficult medical conditions? Maybe you could develop new equipment to treat them. Try biomedical engineering!

- Maybe you'd like to improve the way people make and grow food. You could become an agricultural engineer and work in a lab or on a farm.

- If you want to develop new apps and solve problems with computer systems, think about becoming a software engineer.

Big bridges, deep tunnels, safe buildings . . . those are all fantastic and helpful achievements. But what else do engineers do to improve our lives? How do they make our lives easier and more convenient every day?

Look at the objects above. They're probably very familiar to you. Now, take a moment to think about what they all need in order to work. Did you guess it? **Satellites**! And without engineers, there would be no satellites!

satellite

Some engineers design and build satellites other engineers send them into **orbit**. Engineers must calculate the exact force and direction a satellite needs to get into the right position. If too much force is used, the satellite will keep traveling away from Earth. If not enough force is used, gravity and **air resistance** will pull the satellite down.

Once a satellite is in orbit, it can be used to take photos. It can also help scientists study the earth, the weather, and more. Some satellites receive and send **signals** to and from Earth, too.

Satellite communication happens very fast. In fact, some signals travel at the **speed of light**. This is how you get messages, photos, videos, GPS information, and more from around the world in seconds!

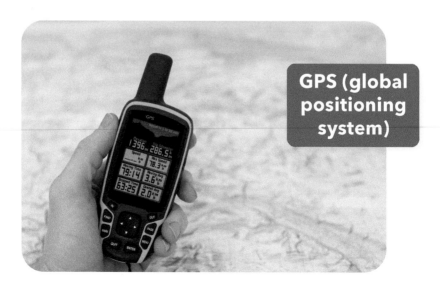

GPS (global positioning system)

signal

space

EXTRA!

Not all satellites orbit Earth. Some satellites orbit the moon or planets. There are even satellites traveling through space, away from Earth. They are not orbiting anything. They will keep going until they lose power. Will they be found by creatures from another planet someday? Who knows? Won't it be interesting to find out?

So, engineers can save us time, make our homes safe, and make our lives easier. But can they really save the world? Maybe!

One huge problem right now is that Earth may be getting warmer as a result of human development. We burn large amounts of fuels like oil and gas, which produce carbon dioxide. Meanwhile, people are cutting down the forests that help to remove CO_2 from the air. This could be creating issues around the world.

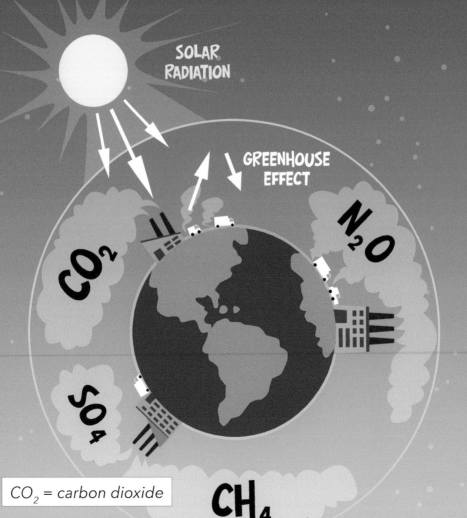

SOLAR RADIATION

GREENHOUSE EFFECT

CO_2

N_2O

SO_4

CH_4

CO_2 = carbon dioxide

Engineers are finding ways to help. They're building machines that can take CO_2 out of the air. This is a good start, but we will need more and bigger machines to completely fix the problem.

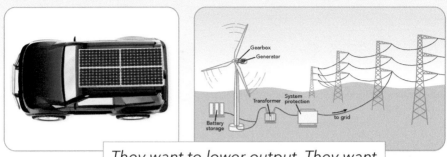

They want to lower output. They want to lower the amount made.

Meanwhile, engineers are also finding ways to reduce CO_2 output. They're building newer, cleaner cars and developing other cleaner forms of energy. This will help put less CO_2 into the air to begin with.

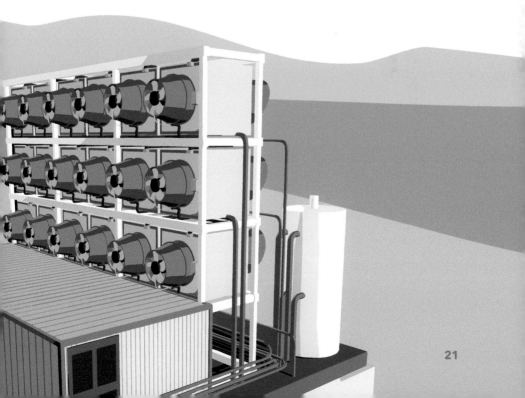

How else can engineers help us in the future? What other problems will they solve? Right now they're looking for ways to clean plastic from our oceans and ways to replace plastic completely. They're coming up with more ways to get clean energy and better ways to store it. They're developing new ways of growing food that are better for the environment. Some engineers are studying how to build better homes. Other engineers are even looking at ways to build homes on the moon or on Mars!

There are so many things that need work!
There are so many ways that engineers
can help. Can engineers find a way? We
think they can. We think they're amazing!

force (*n.*) a power that changes how something moves or does not move or that acts against an object

mass how much there is of an object

motion the action of moving or being moved

investigation the careful study of something, usually to find more information about it or solve a problem

maintain to keep up; to manage and keep in good condition

unbalanced in a state in which something doesn't have the same weight on both sides, which usually causes it to move or fall down

collapse to fall down completely

tension the force that goes through a rope or cable when it is pulled from opposite sides

gravity a force that pulls things to a planet or star

calculation the act of answering a question or solving a problem using numbers, information, and / or math

resist to act against something; to work to stop something

satellite a machine that moves around a planet and collects and sends information

orbit to move around a planet or star

air resistance the force that stops or slows objects traveling through air

signal a radio or other kind of wave that is sent or received for a purpose

speed of light the speed that light moves; 186,282 miles per second (299,792 kilometers per second)